Praise for *Lean Design in Healthcare*

Drama, pride, and professionalism are all chronicled in this new page turner, while the background music belts out pernicious plotting and intrigue. Sounds like a novel but it is life imitating art. Adam Ward has given us a peek inside the looking glass of today's healthcare marketplace. Kudos to Adam for allowing us all to peer in with him.

David B. Nash MD, MBA. Founding Dean
Jefferson College of Population Health, Philadelphia, PA

As healthcare organizations move from provider-centric to patient-centric care models, Adam Ward's Lean Design in Healthcare takes a systems perspective to describe how to redesign your organization and processes. A must-read for anyone interested in transforming healthcare systems.

Aravind Chandrasekaran, Associate Professor and Academic Director (MBOE)
The Ohio State University

Healthcare is undeniably in need of an extreme makeover, with patient-focused innovation at the heart of the solution. What's needed is a practical guide to answering the essential questions of what to do and how to do it. Enter Lean Design in Healthcare. Through a compelling story based on a real-world experience, Adam Ward reveals the principles and practices every health care leader needs to build organizational excellence in innovation.

Matthew E. May, author
The Elegant Solution and Winning the Brain Game

The Healthcare Innovator's Workbook
Making Lean Design in Healthcare Happen

The Healthcare Innovator's Workbook

Making Lean Design in Healthcare Happen

Adam M. Ward

Foreword by Dr. YiDing Yu, Founder of Twiage

Routledge
Taylor & Francis Group

A PRODUCTIVITY PRESS BOOK

First edition published in 2020
by Routledge/Productivity Press
52 Vanderbilt Avenue, 11th Floor New York, NY 10017
2 Park Square, Milton Park, Abingdon, Oxon OX14 4RN, UK

Routledge/Productivity Press is an imprint of Taylor & Francis Group, an Informa business

No claim to original U.S. Government works

Printed on acid-free paper

International Standard Book Number-13: 978-0-367-20144-9 (Hardback)
978-0-367-20140-1 (Paperback)
978-0-429-25974-6 (eBook)

Visit the Taylor & Francis Web site at
http://www.taylorandfrancis.com

Contents

Foreword

I squinted at the small laptop screen. The cool rays of the spring sun in Boston, Massachusetts, filtered through my desk window, while cars hummed by outside. I had just finished our latest fundraiser, bringing in nearly $2 million in seed funding for Twiage. That funding would enable us to grow our team and execute our strategy. In two weeks, I would present our product strategy and road map to the board—decisions that would indelibly write our course for the years to come.

The last year had been challenging but exhilarating. We were signing multihospital deals, growing our revenues, and receiving recognition for our lifesaving innovation, winning top innovation prizes from both the American Medical Association and the Cleveland Clinic. Amazingly, every day more paramedics were choosing Twiage as their standard of communication during a medical emergency. And every day, we had more feature requests roll in.

I knew we had to use our resources wisely. With our small team, every feature we dedicated to development meant another feature would wait on the back burner. Simultaneously, we had to move fast. In a healthcare ecosystem filled with giants, being nimble was one of the few advantages we had. With so many competing needs, how were we going to deploy our capital, and what product road map should I present to the board?

If developing product strategy for a software start-up seems too far removed for your life in healthcare, I must kindly disagree. Granted, as a practicing physician, I had no clue how to be a product owner, much less a venture-funded chief executive officer, until Twiage. But I would put forth to you that healthcare organizations and start-ups have more in common today than ever before. I see our healthcare landscape dramatically evolving before us. Drugstore minute-clinics and stand-alone urgent care centers dot our daily commutes. Hospital and large healthcare organizations are adapting to those competitive pressures, rising costs, and the need to stay ahead of the curve, if not to stay afloat. Unsurprisingly, the tenets of the start-up world and lessons from other industries, like Lean Design, are increasingly leveraged by changemakers in healthcare—changemakers who, like entrepreneurs, must make careful financial decisions and be nimble in the face of giants.

While I've spent nearly my entire professional career as a health tech entrepreneur, I've also served fondly on the other side. Shortly after completing my training in primary care and internal medicine, I served as chief innovation engineer at Atrius Health. Atrius Health is a $2 billion healthcare system in Massachusetts with thirty-six clinical sites and over 900 physicians serving 740,000 primary care patients. It was at Atrius Health where I first met Adam.

Adam Ward was my coach. Our coach, actually. At the Atrius Health Innovation Center, he was a regular presence, teaching us about the Lean Design process and its tools, imparting skills and wisdom along the way. It was through Adam that I first learned about the concept *Obeya*, a Japanese word for "large room." In Lean Design, an obeya tells the story of the project and continually changes to track its progress. My team and I built our own obeya and filled it wall to wall with key insights, learning, charts, graphs, timelines, and tasks. In my role, like in many leadership roles in large organizations, I was often pulled away into meetings, building consensus and buy-in to ensure strategic alignment and implementation success. But every time I returned to my team and our obeya, I found clarity. Alive with color, our obeya tracked complex, year-long projects, reminded us of our learning, and always, always focused on our core vision.

Of course, focus is never easy to maintain. Across my experience in healthcare, I have seen many projects derailed by countless meetings, inevitable squabbles over turf, deference of ownership, or the demands of too many voices. The result is a vision unrealized, a scope skewed, or an amalgamation of different strategies impossible to reconcile and never fully satisfying any—all while wasting precious time, energy, and resources. The larger the organization, the harder it can be to overcome these challenges. Yet start-ups—whether you're an internal innovation team or an entrepreneur—are just as vulnerable. Even small teams with limited resources may have numerous stakeholders—a common refrain in innovation and healthcare. The natural tendency is to become distracted, to forget, through inevitable erosion, where you set off to go. Yet as the leader of your organization, team, or project, ensuring that your team executes toward your core vision is the one thing you can never outsource. I strive to practice it every day, a lesson learned through Adam and realized in our obeya.

This brings me back to that spring day, as I contemplated what Twiage needed to be and how we were going to get there. I had been staring at a blank document on my laptop, waiting for inspiration to hit. I got up and drew out a grid instead. It was a QFD (Chapter 4), populated by everything I knew about our user needs and our value to our customer. The exercise helped us identify the core features that would deliver the most value to our customers and formed the basis of the product road map that informed our strategic decision-making as a company. By focusing and executing that strategic vision, I would lead Twiage to grow by 400% over the next year and establish Twiage as the market leader in the northeast. Eventually, I would launch into my next health tech start-up, taking with me the lessons learned.

Today, I use the skills I learned in the obeya with coach Adam in my everyday work. The lessons of Lean Design are meant to be applied to real problems—problems tackled by changemakers in healthcare who must meet pressing needs with limited resources. These changemakers must be nimble and focused. Having led teams in organizations large and small, I know that these skills come with practice. A companion to Adam's *Lean Design in Healthcare*, this workbook is designed to put Lean Design concepts into practice at your own company. Apply them in your everyday work and execute your core vision. I wish you the best of luck.

YiDing Yu, MD
Founder of Twiage
2018 Cartier Woman Entrepreneur of the Year, North America

Author

Adam M. Ward has an uncanny ability to extract high levels of performance from the teams he works with. He is a natural teacher who breaks down complex topics in the simplest terms. He is an inspirational leader who tells stories with powerful examples that inspire innovative action while staying grounded in the state of the business. He has experience across a multitude of industries, but healthcare became a passion for him, eventually leading him to write the bestselling *Lean Design in Healthcare*, a book about establishing systematic innovation within healthcare organizations. He now runs his own consulting firm.

Just recently, as an Innovation and Strategy Consultant at Simpler (an IBM company), Adam was responsible for executive coaching of the client. Also included on his client list are the U.S. Air Force, Harvard University, Atrius Health, ThedaCare, the U.S. Department of Veterans Affairs, EnerSys, Lockheed Martin, the Gemological Institute of America, Northwestern Mutual, and more. He has established innovation teams, improved product development output, coached C-suites on innovation, and helped develop corporate strategies. After IBM acquired Simpler, he was chosen to create integrated services combining Simpler's proven operational excellence system and IBM's artificial intelligence, Blockchain, and Internet of Things (IoT) technologies.

Previously, as the product development strategist at GE Healthcare, Adam worked for the chief technology officer of the $16 billion company. He was key in creating and implementing multiple, transformative initiatives including the *Product Leader* program for the twelve Diagnostic Imaging divisions and the *Disruptive Cost Workout*, which saved tens of millions of dollars during its launch year and went across other GE units as the standard.

Prior to working at GE Healthcare, Adam was a design leader for Honda R&D Americas. He was responsible for the electrical systems of vehicles, routinely leading cross-functional teams of more than fifty individuals with project capital budgets more than $100 million and material spend exceeding $1 billion annually.

Adam holds an MBA from the Ohio State University and a BSME from the University of Maryland. He has served on several nonprofit boards, led capital campaigns, and speaks regularly at conferences. He has been interviewed by several podcasts and quoted in multiple online publications. An accomplished Ironman with multiple finishes, Adam has competed twice in the Ironman 70.3 World Championships and is an Ultraman World Championship qualifier. He is a student coach and lecturer for the MBOE program at Ohio State.

Introduction

A lot of people asked why *Lean Design in Healthcare* (*LDH*) was written as a fable. Ultimately, it was what the publisher and I thought would be a good introduction to systematic innovation within healthcare. As with any book written as a fictional story, there is so much behind the conversation that takes place. Leadership principles, failures, successes, real-world learning, and more went into why each character was in the story and every line that each character spoke. The advice from the coach is clearly my perspective, taken from what I have seen many times over. Every organization needs the capability to update its portfolio of services on a regular basis. How you do it is up to you. You don't need to reinvent the wheel. Your organization can take this workbook and *LDH* and then plug and play the content.

The book served as an inspiration, but it's not the most practical. This workbook helps make it more practical. It does not stand alone; you still need to read the book. Take both the obvious and not so obvious principles and apply them. The book combines leadership, innovation techniques, healthcare roles, and practical tools. If you need additional help, you can always talk to a coach. Each section can stand alone or work together with the rest of the notebook. Don't rush through it. Use a pencil or make copies (that's why we printed it full-page size). Find someone else to bounce ideas off of and get feedback from.

The workbook works like this: it will refer to the dialogue in *LDH*, ask for points to consider, explain the technical piece, give next-step instructions, and then provide an exercise for you to complete. This will repeat until you've covered every section of the book. Just remember, *LDH* and this workbook are primers to systematic innovation. They are not final, complete solutions. One guarantee though: if you follow both of them, you will be light-years ahead of those who don't. Plus, your providers, staff, and patients will all be happier.

If you're not a top executive, that's OK. I've seen these principles work at every level in an organization. The bigger the organization, the more likely anyone in the healthcare system can do what's in this book. Start with what you control. Get it going there. It'll catch on. It always does.

Introduction

Chapter 1

Players

Systematic innovation is an achievable goal for any organization. Whether you are the chief executive officer (CEO), middle management, or in the early stages of your career, you can make it happen. We face a lot of obstacles in today's environment. Our penchant to spend more than what we have seems to be the major theme, whether that is time or money. Read the titles of these articles:

- A Foolish Take: Here's how much debt the average U.S. household owes https://amp.usatoday.com/amp/107651700
- How Americans' Love Affair with Debt Has Grown https://www.theatlantic.com/business/archive/2010/09/how-americans-love-affair-with-debt-has-grown/63552/
- Americans Are Spending Again: Average American Debt in 2017 https://www.studentdebtrelief.us/news/average-american-debt-2017/
- The Bureau of Labor statistics reports that dual income families are on the rise https://www.bls.gov/news.release/famee.nr0.htm
- Too Many Extracurricular Activities for Kids May Do More Harm Than Good https://psychcentral.com/news/2018/05/15/too-many-extracurricular-activities-for-kids-may-do-more-harm-than-good/135388.html

Unfortunately, our personal habits impact our professional work. We take the same [un] limits in time and money and try to get them to work in our healthcare system. We think there's always more money, always available time, and always available people. But there isn't. And with healthcare costs, healthcare workers' burnout, regulatory dynamism, and consumerism all out of control, it's time to systematize innovation. We need a process that updates healthcare services on a regular basis. The care models we deliver must be radically improved or disrupted. Outsiders think they can do it. Silicon Valley has tried. Disruption will come from within, but an insider will go outside to fix it. Why not be part of the solution now before it's too late and the government forces a solution that is bad for everybody?

Services

Healthcare offers a service to patients: maintaining their health, or their ability to do life. That service is broken into many types of services. Each one of those services is delivered via a care model. Those care models could be a service line like orthopedics or gynecology. They could be delivering routine care, addressing a trauma, or treating something chronic. How we deliver those services determines patient satisfaction. When patients become dissatisfied, they find someone else who can take care of them. As a healthcare system, we want to grow our patient panel, not lose it. Let's look at the totality of services offered as our portfolio of services. We can't let those services get outdated or get behind the competitors. As leaders, we have a small city of employees who depend on us for their livelihood, and we take that responsibility seriously. Nothing ensures the future health outlook of our organization than taking steps to stay healthy today. That includes a constant update of our portfolio. This workbook helps establish that capability.

Some of those services aren't core and are often outsourced so the organization can focus on practicing medicine.

- Clinical (e.g., blood services, dialysis, and lithotripsy)
- Financial (e.g., credit card processing, resource management/staffing, and revenue cycle management)
- Environmental (e.g., facility cleaning, waste management, and linens/laundry)
- Support services (e.g., ambulance, food services, and transcription)

According to research, purchased services can account for up to 35 percent of a typical U.S. hospital's operating expenses. That leaves 65 percent of the budget for care. https://www.beckershospitalreview.com/supply-chain/5-common-misconceptions-about-hospital-purchased-services.html

We have the capability to define every single dollar spent. Our portfolio is a result of our choices. Where we go in the future is up to us, the leaders. Leadership guru John Maxwell defined leadership as "influence." Influence is critical to implementing the principles in this book. https://www.johnmaxwell.com/blog/7-factors-that-influence-influence/

During my time at GE, one of the premier leadership development companies, we were taught a change acceleration process. This allowed us to quickly deploy initiatives across the entire business. A major part required the identification of key stakeholders and whether they were for the change, against it, or neutral. We had a different approach for each categorization. It's critical to have a core group of champions pushing the cause, and it's equally important that you take action against those who are unwilling to change and continue to work against the new direction.

Change expert John Kotter says successful change needs what he calls a "guiding coalition" https://www.kotterinc.com/8-steps-process-for-leading-change/. Many clients ask me what the top failure mode is for Innovation. After having witnessed many successful implementations and many unsuccessful ones, I quickly respond: Lack of active, top leadership support.

Exercise: Identifying and Securing Critical Enablers

Read pages 1–16 of *Lean Design in Healthcare (LDH)*. Here I introduce several characters. These people represent critical roles in making innovation work.

LDH Name	Role	Your Organization
1. _____	_____	_____
2. _____	_____	_____
3. _____	_____	_____
4. _____	_____	_____
5. _____	_____	_____
6. _____	_____	_____
7. _____	_____	_____
8. _____	_____	_____
9. _____	_____	_____
10. _____	_____	_____
11. _____	_____	_____
12. _____	_____	_____
13. _____	_____	_____
14. _____	_____	_____
15. _____	_____	_____
16. _____	_____	_____

As I mentioned in the Introduction, you don't have to be the CEO. Any person at any level can do this. If you're an executive, this should be at your organization. If you're senior management, perhaps this should be at your division. If you're a manager or earlier in your career, it should be in your department. The higher your level, the higher your scope, speed, and success rates.

Ask yourself about your organization. Are there informal leaders, people without a title but with high levels of influence? You want to formalize each of them. Let's list them on the next page. A little caution here, don't share this list with anyone. This is for your eyes only. Use it as a tool to get stuff done and choose whom you want to target with what message.

Stakeholder Analysis

We need a snapshot of our influencers and anti-bodies if we're going to succeed. Who is—and who is not—on our side. Different tactics and communication are required for each. You need to codify the leadership landscape.

Fill out each of the columns. First, identify who the "leader" is. Next, list what things are important to the "leader." What things about work drive that person crazy? In the last two columns, use a High/Medium/Low (H/M/L) rating. One is for level of influence on others, and the other is for level of support

Person	What's Important	What Person Dislikes	Influence Level	Support

On pages 2, 12, and 13 in *LDH*, Mark discusses several issues and opportunities.

What are the top three issues facing your organization?

1. _____

   _____

   _____

   _____

2. _____

   _____

   _____

   _____

3. _____

   _____

   _____

   _____

If you're struggling to narrow it down to three, then write out as many as you consider, and you can use a tool later in the workbook to get the top three (Chapter 3).

Rally Cry

Once you understand your stakeholders and top issues, you have to inspire and mobilize them. This is the best way to influence up. What matters to your boss? Create it here. You might get a promotion out of it. As the leader, you need to develop a concise problem statement that will serve as your rallying cry for innovation. The format of the problem statement should look like this:

[The] Problem is _____ **(some annoying/irritating occurrence or performance); therefore, we must** _____ **(apply this process/countermeasure), so that** _____ **(these results can be achieved).**

Creating a solid problem statement will likely take several iterations. That's OK. In fact, that's usually how the best are formed. Here are some examples of how people create one:

1. Some people initially start with a long paragraph, describing the total situation. Others start with a bulleted list of ideas, problems, and fixes. Put the problem statement away.
2. After reflecting on it, people make a revision or two to the problem statement. Many times, the paragraph gets longer, and the bullet list gets longer. That's OK…for now.
3. They present the problem statement to a close colleague or two, typically someone who will be part of the solution in some way or another. The problem statement might get picked apart here. That's good. At this point, it is best to make sure that the paragraph or list is clear and concise and not lengthy.
4. Another revision is made prior to the first team meeting, and it is sent to team members before the meeting.
5. After a brief introduction to the background and direction, the problem statement is presented. The goal here is ratification. This usually means strong, healthy discussion. Individual words are debated until everyone in the room is happy with what it says.

The problem statement might not be final at this point, but it should be 95 percent there. Resist the urge to allow people to come to you individually later for suggestions and changes. They had a chance to discuss it in the meeting. Propose changes only in a group meeting.

The following is a template to track the evolution of your own problem statement. Remember, the problem statement serves as your rally cry. A strong rally cry galvanizes teams and resolve. Try it on the next page.

Rally Cry Evolution

[The] Problem is _____ (some annoying/irritating occurrence or performance); therefore, we must _____ (apply this process/ countermeasure), so that _____ (these results can be achieved).

First Draft
Problem:

Action Needed:

Results Desired:

Revision(s)
Problem:

Action Needed:

Results Desired:

Ratified Version
Problem:

Action Needed:

Results Desired:

Succinct Statement:

In addition to the statement, it's helpful to have an idea of what we're wanting to leave behind and what the future could look like. Let's do some reflection and some dreaming. In alignment with your rally cry, describe what today feels like and what tomorrow could feel like. Draw a picture, stick figures encouraged, that captures the essence of each.

Vision Casting

Rally Cry:

Now

■ _____

■ _____

■ _____

Draw image here

Future

■ _____

■ _____

■ _____

Draw image here

Celebration Dinner

Far too many managers and executives skip this part of the process. They don't take the time to celebrate. This is becoming even more critical with younger generations entering the workforce. Don't shake your head at this, always have a reason to throw a party.

Read pages 14–15 in *LDH*. I buried a couple of nuances in the text there.

What sticks out to you?

_____

_____

_____

At the bottom of page 14 in *LDH*, I talk about the Innovation team's celebration dinner. Instead of a steakhouse or chart house, they went with a nontraditional ethnic food. This is a small homage to a willingness to experiment and engage with a culture different than our own. Some people, having grown up or going to college in a diverse area, were more willing to branch out. Others who have lived in a homogenous society for most of their lives may find greater difficulty exploring the differences. An initial probe into the differences may further cement one's views on being inclusive or not. Check out the following example.

I live in a metropolitan area with over 2 million people. In the seven-county area, there are over 1100 churches. One Sunday, I decided to visit two distinctly different churches on the same morning. The first one was a traditional, black, inner-city church, while the second was a relatively new one in an affluent suburb that was virtually all white.

Since I grew up in a church that was diverse and urban, I knew what to expect. I was dressed in full suit and tie but was definitely outdressed by the ushers, deacons, and most of the older attendees. In a sanctuary holding more than 1000 congregants, I was one of less than five white people. The singing, preaching, and audience participation felt like it was at a fever pitch the entire time. If I wasn't clapping, standing, or shouting, I wasn't fitting in. It was Black History Month, and the pastor suggested that next weekend everyone "kente up" (kente is colorfully patterned cloth, traditionally African) our clothes, including the "white folk," as a sign of celebration and unity.

Church two was quite different. I ditched my tie and walked in. My suit made me way overdressed. Most people wore jeans, including the pastor. As I looked around the room, hundreds of suburbanites were holding cups of their flavored coffee. There was almost zero participation or excitement from the crowd during the entire service, yet everyone seemed engaged. There were very few

African Americans in the younger audience, and Black History Month was never mentioned. Suicide was the topic of the day.

Although both services included a time of singing, a time of preaching, and the requisite offering, they couldn't have seemed more different. However, the attendance suggested that both were thriving religious organizations.

The 2016 election made xenophobia a common term. While I don't think most of us are truly afraid of those different than us, there is definitely a comfort level associated with familiarity. We tend to spend time with those similar to us. When it comes to innovation, xenophobia gives us tunnel vision. Venturing into the unknown is the first step. We must learn to immerse ourselves in new situations on a nearly constant basis. Here's an exercise to help.

Take a few minutes and reflect on yourself.

Which culture do you spend the most time in?

Look at the food you ate in the past three months, one year, ten years. How many times did you try something new? Make a list of new foods that you have discovered or want to discover.

What people groups do you spend your free time with? What is the diversity in age, gender, ethnicity, and belief systems? Which ones would be quite convenient between your place of work and where you live to discover and become a part of?

What do you think about celebration? How often do you take time to formally celebrate wins? Is there a favorite way for your team to celebrate? What could you do to make celebration a core value?

In the last couple of paragraphs on page 13 in *LDH*, I talked about ridesharing, a recent business model that has almost completely eliminated the [horrible] taxi experience. Ten years ago, who would've guessed that anybody with a four-door sedan or SUV could get approval from a company to earn money while driving complete strangers around. Two years ago, I got my Uber XL certification so I could pick up and drop off people. It wasn't for money; it was so that I could experience culture from the chauffeur's seat. In a single weekend, I saw the widest variety of people and situations that I had in years. I haven't driven since then, and my certification has lapsed, but it goes to show how something that started as an idea in a strategy session years ago in Silicon Valley ended up as a tool for ethnography in the Midwest. We are surrounded by new innovations that can raise our insights into the diversity of whom we serve, we just have to choose to engage.

Chapter 2

Basics

In the innovation process, there is both art and science. Art requires imagination and creativity. Science requires discipline and adherence. Each are critical to systematic success. Let me share with you a personal example.

While writing this workbook, I visited a client in the town of my undergraduate alma mater. I hadn't been on the engineering campus in over 20 years, so I decided to drive through it the night before my meeting.

I was having fond flashbacks of our team's solar car lab and the machine shop where theory became reality. I could also recall the harsh study weeks of every semester, taking difficult classes but simply wanting to design things. The lab was an escape for me. It was where I could build and experiment. To me, being an inventor was everything. It's what I enjoyed and what I wanted to do. From the time I was a child until this day, I have a penchant for recognizing improvement opportunities, seeing patterns, and creating solutions. There were no better times for me than when I imagined something in my head and worked to make it a reality. It was the final outcome that drove me through the frustrating building period. The pinnacle of satisfaction was when the project was completed, and I could fully interact with what I had created. I loved the art of innovation, and although I enjoyed the engineering calculations, I hated the science of the innovation process. Following graduation, I began designing cars for Honda R&D Americas. I found a strictness in process that I had never seen or experienced in innovation. In my early days, I rebelled against the process, accepting it only as a means to the part I really enjoyed, the problem-solving from concept to reality. However, as time went on, I began to recognize and appreciate the beauty of the process. The process freed me from wasting precious brain power on what to do next, what the order was, or what things had been tried in the past. If I was doing the appropriate art portion at each stage of the science portion, what I was creating would be excellent. Those times when I ignored the process, I often had to spend heavy rework on the art. Like a Yogi demonstrating the perfect crane pose, I had to find my perfect balance.

I have found that true innovators are not only drawn to but thrive in the art portions of innovation. They love the idea generation, the trade-off decisions, the quest for something unique and helpful. They are drawn to the unknown. I have also seen many successful innovators who are drawn to the process of innovation. They love the discipline and opportunity to flex their organizational and planning abilities. Checklists appeal to them.

Every great inventor, every iconic artist, and every brilliant musician masters both the art and the science. *Lean Design in Healthcare* (*LDH*) is far more about the science than it is the art. It's about creating a construct in which innovation can thrive. The book gives a predictable pathway that both innovators and noninnovators, staff and providers, entry level workers and executives can enjoy and use. Learning and mastering the science can unlock a new level of repetitive innovation, becoming a core strategic advantage in successfully achieving your mission and becoming the default choice of patients in your geographic area.

Take a couple of minutes and read pages 17–19 at the beginning of Chapter 2 in *LDH*. There are a few key concepts that need to be pulled out here.

First, note that the coach is called "the expert." You need access to an expert. Make sure this is not a wannabe expert. Big caution to you here: don't hire an expert who hasn't actually done complete innovation. When you're looking for an expert to hire, make sure you choose one who has actually designed, who holds patent(s), and who has gone through the entire development cycle several times. I have encountered numerous people over the years who have never done actual innovation, yet they claim to know the answers for product or service development. Honestly, their tools are probably better than nothing, but they're very limited in their performance level. Accordingly, it comes nowhere close to world class. Do yourself a favor, and hire someone who has done it. It's a higher initial investment, but your health system will make more money or save more money as a result.

The next piece to pay attention to is the "just hire them or develop them." A lot of executives balk at the cost of a consultant and say, "we could afford multiple FTEs for the price of this consultant." It is true, you can hire multiple full-time equivalents (FTEs). However, you're still not going to have the expertise you need. Can you imagine someone saying, "Hire a couple of college students and try to teach them to be doctors in the emergency department." It's quite similar (minus the board certifications). Eventually, they could learn what they need, but it's going to be a while. It's the same for innovation skills; it's about a ten-year journey for most engineers.

Another area in *LDH* was subtle that needs highlighting is the patient who dramatically changed his health trajectory. This is a frequent example of comparing personal health transformation with corporate transformations. It's very easy for people to go into the doctor's office, hear them say "diet and exercise," and then do nothing afterward. Most significant lifestyle changes seem to be a result of an exacerbation. However, there are plenty of people who are able to achieve it without a heart attack or a stroke. Learning to be innovative, having a process to do so, and achieving good results is a lot like a health transformation. There are a significant number of habits that need to be changed. Some of them are different, and they can be painful to begin with. However, just like a regular regimen for diet and exercise, innovation can become second nature, and future health can radically improve.

There is an important phrase right in the middle of page 18 in *LDH*. It says, "Minimize the amount of time we use him by maximizing our rate of learning." A couple of paragraphs later, it talks about "overall cost we are investing." These paragraphs talk about the amount of time you need to seek outside expertise. You could run anywhere on the spectrum from needing someone full-time for a long time to partial FTE needing spot checks. The overall cost of innovation needs to be looked at with its own return on investment (ROI). Too many organizations, that clearly don't have the internal capability, are also unwilling to pay for someone to teach them. This simply does not get you where you need to be.

More often than not, there is a disproportionate amount of scrutiny placed on the cost of the consultant and not on the process or learning rate of the company. Let's face it, when undergoing a "transformation," it requires a different way of doing things. Sometimes you know what to do, but many times you don't. Get someone who knows what they're doing and learn as fast as you can. Whoever that person is, he or she needs to be close with the CEO. In *LDH*, Marc knows that if he isn't actively engaged, Angstrom Health will not achieve its goals.

Take a few minutes and jot down a couple of notes on this section.

How much internal capability do you have?

What size is your team?

Who can you hire?

What outside help do you need?

How much are you willing to spend?

How long do you think it will take?

The answers to these questions will guide you. Perhaps they caused more questions. Either way, you're learning and moving forward strategically and not randomly. There will be more on this in Chapter 2 of *LDH*.

Terminology

The definition of innovation is discussed on pages 19–24 in *LDH*. Please read these pages before continuing.

As one of my coworkers used to say, "I don't care if you call *it* innovation or cucumber, but you need to agree on the definition." The biggest need for a definition is so that everybody on the leadership team and the innovation core team are headed toward the same goal. You don't want to get 6–12 months in and have somebody ask, "I thought this is what we meant." Unfortunately, this happens far too many times, and there is nothing but frustration among everyone involved.

Over my years of consulting in this space, I have seen 100 definitions of what companies think innovation is. In fact, everybody has a definition, but very few are actually doing it. There is an entire discussion among innovation communities about what should be called "innovation": incremental or disruptive? With the definition in the book, it's clear: Innovation is the output of a process that creates a disruptive product or service, simultaneously obsoleting the status quo. Allow me to explain the rationale behind each portion of the definition. When I am done explaining, then you have to do the hard work of creating the agreed definition for your organization.

I say "hard work" because it's easy for one person to create his own definition based on the culture of the organization and where he thinks the organization is headed. To get an entire team of leaders to agree to the definition takes some effort. It won't get done in a single session. Now, you could get it done in a single session, but the long-term quality can come back to bite you in the end. The problem is not the words but the tie to strategy and how the definition helps achieve it.

Definition

Instead of focusing on incremental or disruptive, consider the word "obsolete." Therein lies the key. An innovation makes prior choices no longer acceptable to the consumer. The consumer could be internal (provider, clinician, nurse) or external (patient, caregiver, family member). If it's just another choice, it's not an innovation. As we go further through the book, we see the importance of the process and how it ensures that it's not just another choice, but it is a replacement.

Think of some examples of real world improvement versus obsolescence.

_____ versus _____

_____   _____

_____   _____

_____   _____

_____   _____

_____   _____

_____   _____

_____   _____

What "innovations" actually made work harder for the provider or patient?

_____

_____

_____

What innovations have made life better?

_____

_____

_____

Which innovations are your peers at other hospitals using that you don't have at your system?

_____

_____

_____

Use the boxes below, or grab some stickies. Write out elements of your definition for presentation to your company. In the background, my original definition is in light gray. Even if you choose to use it, copy the words in your own handwriting.

Innovation is the output of a process that creates a disruptive product or service, simultaneously obsoleting the status quo.

Special Lean Section

Prior to this section, please read the Lean subsection that starts at the bottom of page 20 in *LDH*.

I reluctantly accepted the title of my book to include the term "Lean" in it. I honestly felt like that term had run its course, and that the shiny object syndrome would no longer let visionaries pick up a publication with that term in the name. However, Eric Riese's work with *The Lean Startup* showed that Lean still has legs. Many practitioners of Lean, outside of thought leadership firms, are shifting to "operational excellence" as their preferred term. Whether "Lean" is trendy or not, *Lean Design* is *very* different than *Operational Lean* or the *Toyota Production System*. I use the prefix "operational" to differentiate basic Lean principles from Lean Design. There is a myriad of books on Lean. With a handful of exceptions, they are about Lean in an operations setting.

There have been a significant number of heated debates between Lean Design and Operational Lean practitioners regarding the differences and applicability of each.

Warning: Do not be fooled by Operational Lean practitioners thinking that their principles are good for innovation. They.are.not.

Anyone who tells you otherwise has never been an innovator and most likely came out of some type of manufacturing background. I have seen time and time again Operational Lean team members ruining innovation efforts. In fact, the more experienced they are in Operational Lean, the worse they are. In healthcare, this problem becomes even more magnified. Too many practitioners are trying to turn healthcare into assembly lines, essentially ignoring the art, unpredictability, and customized treatment plans of medicine. Granted, there are repeatable, predictable processes in healthcare. Lab services, patient registration, revenue cycle, and inpatient medication are a few examples where Operational Lean can yield tremendous results. However, any physician can tell you that standard appointment times for every patient never work. Those practicing in primary care can tell you about the big difference between Mondays and Fridays or the impact weather can have on appointments. Operational Lean is built on a foundation of [relative] predictability. The goal is zero waste and zero variation. Wastes include waiting, transportation, movement, inventory, overproduction, overprocessing, and rework. Anytime a step in the process is paused, a mistake is made, more than the necessary amount is produced, or more than the minimal materials are stocked, people walk back and forth or reach too far, waste exists.

Operational Lean practitioners push standard operating procedures for every activity. They want to define time, number of units, number of people, distance traveled, and acceptable "scrap" for every process step from trigger to done. Any variation from the standard is unacceptable, and reoccurrence requires team-based problem-solving and countermeasures.

That being said, if it fits the appropriate parameters, there is no other methodology that improves operations better than Lean. Period. Quality is vastly better. Cost is minimized. Capacity is improved. Employee satisfaction goes up. I have seen countless examples of radical improvement through implementation of Lean principles. Here is a simple way of determining if

Operational Lean should be used:

- Does a process currently exist?
- Is the process repeated many times daily?
- Is there latent frustration by staff or patients?
- Does the process have critical safety/quality steps?

If any of these exist, you can use Operational Lean.

Meanwhile, here are a few things to consider using Lean Design:

- No process yet exists
- Need a quantum jump in performance
- Desire differentiation from competitors
- Have a new technology or service

Take a few minutes to think about issues in your practice that need improvement.

Issue	Type of Lean

It may take a few times before it gets easy to identify issues and determine what type of Lean techniques are needed. If the bulk of your issues say Lean Design, let's keep going. If not, there are a number of great Operational Lean books for healthcare, including the following:

- *The Lean Prescription* by Patty Gabow
- *On the Mend* by John Toussaint
- *Lean Hospitals* by Mark Graban
- *Lean Healthcare* by Marc Hafer

Now that we have established our definition for innovation and provided an explanation between Lean Design and Operational Lean, we can move forward. Read pages 23–24 in *LDH*. There are three areas required for successful, systematic innovation.

List them here:	What it means to you/your organization
1.	
2.	
3.	

This is one of the first areas where administration pushes back. They love the thought of innovation, can't wait to beat St. Whoever Health, and want to control costs, but they don't want to do the work.

Imagine practicing medicine without that list of three things. It simply wouldn't work.

Now, don't get me wrong, innovation can happen in the absence of those three things, but *systematic* innovation cannot. If you have a single area that needs innovation, I would recommend running a design thinking workshop (see page 128 in *LDH*) and use Agile project management to deliver it. (Yes, I just gave you a major shortcut to this whole book. But it's single use only.)

Again, we're after systematic, repeatable innovation. We want one innovation after another, repeatedly, to constantly offer better services and experiences for our patients.

The last thing we want is to become obsolete ourselves.

Take some time and really think about these questions. Write down your top reflections.

What would happen to our patients if we were acquired or became bankrupt?

What competitors want our patients?

What are they doing that we aren't?

What is the impact of retail clinics, outpatient surgical centers, or urgent care on us?

What is the likelihood of us becoming obsolete in the next 15 years? Why or why not?

Read the subsection at the bottom of page 29 in *LDH*.

How often do you update your active patient list?

What is the population growth in your area?

How are you matching it?

How are you doing analytics on the patients and their appointment types?

There may be a shift in behavior due to competitors. Just because you have the same number of patients on your list doesn't mean you're winning. There could be turnover or "one and done," both signs of obsolescence.

Before we get into the list of three, let's talk about how we will measure performance. Physicians remind me of professional athletes. They have an extremely strong desire to win. They are highly competitive. The scoreboard is critical. Most people perform better when winning is defined, but healthcare is fanatical about it.

Useful, meaningful metrics drive systematic innovation. Read pages 24–26 and 30 in *LDH*. In the first few paragraphs, the leader asks which metrics should be measured. Unfortunately, there is no silver-bullet metric. Many people want to record the number of ideas or the time it took to launch a project. While these are good to know, they aren't the metrics that I would focus on. Let's look back to our definition for innovation. Remember, we want *repeatable* innovation. I recommend having metrics for the process and metrics for the output. We need metrics that can be reviewed and discussed monthly. Ones that can't vary that frequently shouldn't be on the scoreboard (e.g., weekly A1C). If they remain static from quarter to quarter, you need new metrics. I also recommend limiting the number of metrics because too many organizations become paralyzed tracking metrics. The activity drifts toward becoming the metrics and nothing else. With metrics, to start off, you could use these:

■ Percentage of innovation basics in place
■ Adherence to innovation framework
■ Number of meaningful opportunities identified
■ Robustness of governance

If you don't have a standard in place, then you don't have a process. We need a process for systematic innovation. Early metrics should be few and around the process. Eventually, you can introduce metrics related to time, quality, financial aspects, and quantity of projects. We are not ignoring those—they will just be at a project level.

It's important that the metrics flow up to the next tier of management. People working on the projects should know how they are impacting the ones that are being presented to the executives. Everyone should understand how winning is defined. Executives should be prepared to remove barriers that enable winning. Discussions about subpar performance should not be about why we're doing poorly, but what needs to be done to succeed. It's far too easy just to get into a finger-pointing, blaming match instead of focusing on what needs to be done to be successful. Dysfunctional teams blame; high-performance teams figure out how. You can likely come up with a list of metrics, but you might want to consider consulting an expert for these. It's easy to drive the wrong behavior as a result of poor ones.

Let's talk about the first things needed to start systematic innovation: the team, workspace, and governance. (Basic tools and the innovation framework will each get their own chapter.) We'll start with the team.

Team

The team is simply a group of people who will be responsible for systematic innovation. Read pages 31–37 in *LDH*. Here I give examples of characters, what roles they play on the team, and how involved they are. The ingredients for the team recipe have an almost infinite amount of variations. Like metrics, there is no single best practice. However, I want to distill the critical points that are a must for every team:

1. Dedicated leader
2. Full-time innovator(s)
3. Cross-functional representation
4. Information technology (IT) support

Numbers 1 and 2 must be full time. The others can range from as needed (PRN) to full time based on the need. This becomes a defining moment for organizations. Many places don't have hiring slots for nonclinical FTEs nor are they willing to shift people out of operations. If things are so bad you can't free up two to three people, you don't need this book. I've walked away from many potential clients on this single issue. They wanted me to get it to work by adding innovation responsibility to their existing roles. This has been tried many times. What did I learn? It's impossible for systematic innovation and nearly impossible for single innovations. People can't add something else to their schedule. Something always suffers. The loudest boss gets their way, almost always to the detriment of innovation. Caveat: There are no dual roles unless you are removing existing responsibility to make room for innovation.

The Leader

Executive teams always ask, "what requirements do we need for the *ideal* leader?" When *ideal* qualities are listed, there are usually blank stares accompanied by, "We don't have someone like that." It's OK, we don't need *ideal*. Here are the attributes that are the most critical in order of importance:

■ Pioneering resilience
■ Networked and respected
■ Healthcare economic knowledge

Ideally, this person should report to the CEO or president, at least for a short-term basis. It is highly discouraged to put this person under operations (chief operating officer [COO]). The monthly, quarterly, or annual financials will always get in the way. Also, a dyad leadership that doesn't like the changes has a higher chance of shutting down the innovation.

Another person they shouldn't report to is the chief information officer (CIO). Their focus is almost always on the electronic medical record (EMR) or something related to next-generation software solutions. CIOs have a tendency to lead with the solution instead of the need.

Innovators

These people seem to be more successful when they are earlier in their career or come from outside of healthcare. There are two reasons for this: they haven't experienced the career-long beatdown of having ideas rejected, and they provide outside objectivity in an environment in which one role usually calls all of the shots.

Humility, curiosity, and a penchant for iterative design are the most desired qualities for these people. Depending on the size of the team, it is preferred that one of the innovators have some administrative capability for documenting and creating the formal process. That type of person may be less creative but will nevertheless help ensure the development of an innovation framework and that it is being followed. If the search is done internally, these people can be found in a wide variety of existing healthcare roles from medical secretary to surgeon. Remember, however, that their salary will contribute directly to the cost of the innovation team. Ideally this team is made up of a mix of internal and external candidates. If you could get one designer and one engineer on the team, it would be extremely beneficial. They have the training to generate ideas, assess feasibility, and produce an actual solution.

Many organizations want to know how big the team needs to be. That depends on how big the organization is and the number of disruptions that need to be created. Innovation teams at the Cleveland Clinic, Mayo Clinic, and UPMC number over 100 people. Those may seem like impossible numbers, but they started at zero at one point as well. There seems to be a critical mass of five full-timers. Less than that, and the initiative typically dies.

Once the leader is chosen, a charter must be created for the innovation team. This includes budget, metrics, and expectations. The executive leadership team (ELT) should approve the charter before proceeding. Anything less than a year is fraught with problems. A good time frame to consider is 1–3 years. The budget needs to cover people, space, and money for projects (e.g. equipment, software, and experiments). Consider funding from a foundation if your health system has one. You should target an ROI greater than five. Once the budget is set, a project can be chosen by the leader, and the team can be determined. Sometimes groundwork must be done before a project is chosen. In this case, fill the innovator position(s) first.

Provider

Anyone with an MD/DO behind their name will greatly impact the budget. On top of that, it usually means taking them away from seeing patients.

However, nothing establishes credibility like having a doctor on the team. If the leader is a physician, an advanced practice clinician (APC) may be the best choice. Someone with more than 10 years in the role does well.

Take a few minutes and make a short list of people that you would think what do good at leading innovation. What is their score on each of the three? Use high, medium, and low.

Name	Pioneer	Network	Economics	Comments

It would be a shame to put someone in this position who is just a puppet for one of the members of the executive leadership team.

Other Roles

There are a variety of other roles mentioned in the book. It is not meant to be exhaustive but instead representative of what innovation centers have generally used on a variety of projects while talking next-generation health. These are basic roles that should have some representation. As mentioned on pages 26–27 in *LDH*, the amount of effort varies for these roles. They can range anywhere from curbside advice to full time. Generally speaking, if the role is important to the project, they should be dedicating at least 20 percent of their time to the team. Less than that and they risk being disconnected from the core team and poorly representing their function back to their peers. With the prominence of the digital age, you need to have someone on the team who can pull information out of your data warehouse. You also need someone who can work with the EMR. Too many times, innovation teams have ground to a halt because of an absence of these two positions. The more serious the innovation team effort becomes, the more you should consider making one or more of these roles a permanent full-time position on the team.

It's always smart to include a nurse and someone related to mental health. They spend a significant amount of time with patients in their most vulnerable state and are expert listeners. They are on the front lines and interact with the patient and their loved ones, giving them an unparalleled peek into what's needed and what works.

There is a big statement on the performance excellence team member in *LDH*. As previously mentioned in the Operational Lean versus Lean Design section, there needs to be clear boundaries. Performance excellence team members have a tendency to think purely about operations. While this is critical later in the project stages, it has a tendency to kill great ideas early on. More times than not, they suck the creativity out of the team and focus purely on process. Consider yourself warned if you decide to make this person part of the extended or full-time team. The best practice is to involve them during the middle to end stages of the RED (research, exploration, delivery) framework (Chapter 4 in this workbook).

Let's talk about the diversity of the team. The last thing you want is homogeneity. The higher the diversity, the better … IF … they can work together as a team. If this is difficult, at least try to balance the male-to-female ratio as evenly as possible.

Now, with all this being said, let's think about how to start. Every innovation team should be formed based on one or more projects, never in a vacuum or in the absence of a project. The leaders should have the dominant say in who joins the team. They are the ones who will be working with them on a daily basis. With that being said, there is usually a negotiation with the executive leadership team to discuss which team members would need to be pulled from the various functions and to what extent. The leader should prepare a list of candidates and functions only after a project is chosen.

The team may feel a little clunky at the beginning as they are getting used to working with each other while simultaneously working with a higher level of ambiguity. It is critical during this time that the leader monitor the cohesiveness of the team and the impact individual members are having on that. Everyone should know that they have a 3- to 6-month probation time. Yes, at any time the leader senses an individual doesn't appear to be working, the leader needs to remove that member from the team. Please do not second-guess this. Go with your intuition. Nothing ruins an innovation team faster than one team member who can't get along with the others. You are doing yourself a huge disservice by keeping that person on board. In fact, you may jeopardize the entire team. If you made a mistake, get rid of the person quickly. Have a 90-day probation period. Use it. Don't wait until the end to have a conversation with that person about not fitting in so they can just temporarily adjust behavior and say they'll work on it. Move quickly.

Core Team

Use this page to brainstorm potential people for each of the roles mentioned here.

Role	Who might do well	Why?
_____	_____	_____
_____	_____	_____
_____	_____	_____
_____	_____	_____
_____	_____	_____
_____	_____	_____
_____	_____	_____
_____	_____	_____
_____	_____	_____
_____	_____	_____
_____	_____	_____
_____	_____	_____

Space

The worst-case scenario for an innovation team would be the following: part time and working from their existing desks. Like every other function, innovators need a space that is functional for their activities. Many organizations balk at giving a team a new space. You don't need a Google campus, but you do need something.

Innovation Space

1. What spaces are available?

2. How many people can meet/work there?

3. What length of time can you occupy the space?

The last sentence at the bottom of page 38 in *LDH* is critical. It underlines the importance of having to keep relationships close. It's the only way to maintain a lever for barrier removal. This can be done a variety of ways but is best achieved in social settings or impromptu hallway meetings that don't have an agenda.

Operating Mechanisms

Pages 39, 44–45, and 50 in *LDH* talk about the ideal amount of iteration and Agile versus stage gate processes. If you aren't up to speed on either of these methodologies, there are a number of articles online that can give you base knowledge. If you want a deeper dive, here are a couple of recommended books:

■ *Agile Project Management with Scrum* by Ken Schwaber
■ *Scrum: The Art of Doing Twice the Work in Half the Time* by Jeff Sutherland

Agile was created for software. Software is not a service, although it delivers one. Software is typically programmed by young people who are digitally native. Software doesn't care about quality or safety. Software has reached an unacceptable level with too many releases.

You can open your phone's app store and see the number of updates recently installed or waiting to be installed on your phone. The number is mind-boggling. Unfortunately, over 80 percent of the updates are to fix bugs. Agile Sprint methodology attempts to release software updates every week or two. Consultants in the Agile community are trying to get Agile techniques applied to every other industry. The main problem is releasing a new service is quite different then updating software. Could you imagine retraining your medical teams every month, let alone weekly? That would be silly. You have to be intentional with the releases that change workflows. These should be considered monumental: personnel changes, new software implementation, or new facilities. We don't get a chance to "fix the bugs." That could mean harm or poor care for the patient. The designs that come out of your process must be robust from the introduction.

Pages 40–44 in *LDH* discuss innovation governance. This is an area with a significant number of opinions and practices. LDH has boiled multiple best practices down to the basics for healthcare and others:

■ Master schedule
■ Team meetings
■ Work wall

It's amazing what a list of tasks and cross-functionally attended meetings can do for keeping projects on task. In fact, as stated in the middle of page 40 in *LDH*, you are likely doubling the length of your project if you don't have these two simple things in place. This list of three includes those two.

Master Schedule

Picking a release date is like picking a wedding date—it doesn't move. You have to decide what is important and what trade-offs have to be made along the way.

The master schedule is not a Gantt chart, but it is a visual display of the major sections and deadlines of the project from beginning to end. Iterations occur within the master schedule.

In the middle of page 45 in *LDH*, there is a discussion about the length of each stage. You need to understand what your organization's "cycle of impatience" is. This is the length of time that executives become tired of asking the same question over and over about when it's going to be done. Every organization has a different length. You want your master schedule to fall within that timeline. Ideally, 1 year or more would be great. If it's less than that, the amount of change you will be able to create will be incremental, and the sizes of your projects will have to be scoped down accordingly. Let's try it on the next page.

Master Schedule

Take any major event and map it below. This could be a vacation, a party, a work event or anything that has a fixed day it happens.

Project

Major Tasks	Beginning	Middle	End
1. _____			
2. _____			
3. _____			
4. _____			
5. _____			
6. _____			

Roughly place the major tasks on the overall timeline. Now you have your master schedule. Of course, there may be some adjustments to when the major tasks are done, but the end date doesn't change.

As you may notice, some of the later tasks are dependent on earlier tasks. We'll discuss this more during the work wall section.

Team Meetings

Read pages 45–48 in *LDH*, paying attention to the main debate points between the coach and the team. What stood out to you?

_____

_____

_____

_____

_____

How are your meetings currently run?

What would your ideal meeting look and feel like?

What is the difference between what you do today and your ideal meeting?

Why?

What proposal or idea can you make to shift your meetings more like those in the book?

Work Wall

Simply implementing pages 48–50 in *LDH* alone could be a game changer for your organization. It is one of the most powerful tools for teams and executives. Let's take an example from your personal or professional life and populate the three sections on the next page.

Three Bins

Think about what you've done the past 2 weeks, what you're working on right now, and what you have to be working on over the next few weeks.

Write them down in the appropriate column. Don't put them in the completed column unless they are completely finished. Don't put items in the middle column if you haven't started to spend time on them yet.

Queue   **WIP (work in process)**   **Complete**

_____   _____   _____

_____   _____   _____

_____   _____   _____

How does the distribution look?

Are there too many things for you to be working on simultaneously? Does your work in progress look like rush hour on the highway? Are there an overwhelming number of things waiting to be worked on?

If so, you're trying to do too much with too few resources. The same goes for your team. Just having this on display will allow team members, the leader, and executives see the amount of work.

The Harvey Ball

Next to each item on the previous page, add a Harvey ball, and fill it out for each based on this rubric:

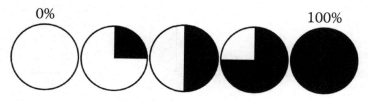

0%—No work done
25%—Some thought given with plan
50%—Action taken
75%—Strong effort (almost done)
100%—Complete (not "almost" done)

Sticky Note Basics

Finally, you will notice that things will move from left to right based on what stage they are. The easiest way to do this is to write each item on a sticky note and move it when appropriate.

A sticky note should have four basic things included: the task or learning, the approximate due date, the level of completion, and the responsible person.

Here is an example of a sticky note. There are teams that have color-coded sticky notes for different functions or types of learning and other teams that use random colors. Best practices limit the description of the task to less than seven words. They also use a fine-tip marker like a Sharpie.

There are a few things to think about. Let's go back to our wedding example or, if you prefer, a fly-fishing trip. From the date of engagement to the wedding day or the trip day, the schedule is fixed. There are some items that have a longer time to get ready. Determining the venue/lodge and its availability is usually the first thing. Getting the dress or the gear can take time as well. We want to make sure that we are doing things in the right order and not just grabbing them randomly from the overall list of tasks. If someone is unsure about how long something will take, a flag should be raised. Missed schedules and launch dates that could have been avoided had we known the lead time and the order of the major tasks or learnings are basic skills. If the team is new, it may not know them yet. Someone should be assigned to recording how long it takes so that the second time through the process there are no surprises. As time goes on, we should try to shrink the length of time as much as possible. This will allow us to complete projects at a faster rate.

Now, let's take a look at some tools that help us in the innovation process.

Chapter 3

Basic Tools

The previous chapter was the #StopEatingFrenchFries and the #MoveNaturally method of getting in better shape. Without intake control, physical movement, and an elevated heart rate, you won't achieve better health. Ditto for innovation. (This will be a favorite section of the workbook for those who have a proclivity for tool usage.) My big warning here is that this is just a beginner set and that systematic innovation is far beyond a set of tools. These tools should become integrated in every project and meeting your team has. It should become the way you do work, make decisions, and ensure innovation process quality. Just like physical tools, they are enablers for better work.

Read pages 51–52 in *Lean Design in Healthcare* (*LDH*). Do you have a formalized tool for any of the following seven?

1. Team communication   Y/N
2. Meeting notes   Y/N
3. Patient focus   Y/N
4. Pugh matrix   Y/N
5. Queue   Y/N
6. Analytical hierarchy process (AHP)   Y/N
7. Failure modes and effects analysis   Y/N

Team Communication

Poor communication is the second failure mode for major initiatives, only behind lack of leadership support. Leaders cannot repeat the vision, mission, and direction enough. In fact, it should be their main job. The team must communicate as well. As mentioned on page 52 in *LDH*, there are three ways to focus on team communication.

Read pages 52 and 53 in *LDH*. What stands out to you?

_____

_____

_____

When you think about your communication, answer these questions:

How does your team communicate, officially and unofficially?

What do team members think are the proper channels for communication?

What is your thought on those methods being the best way for sharing information and keeping up to date?

How would your organizational policy around communication need to change to improve effectiveness?

What does it need to add or modify?

Who can you talk to about it?

How do you talk to your friends? Your significant other? Family members?

What's different talking with them than work colleagues?

Caution: Don't feel the pressure to go buy some enterprise communication tool. Don't join a bandwagon simply because others are. For example, as of this writing, Slack is a very popular team communication software. Quite honestly, I have found it clunky and difficult to use; it's overkill for small teams, and it can add a ton of distractions. Keep it simple, as simple as you can. As with anything in healthcare, make sure that you are not discussing Health Insurance Portability and Accountability Act (HIPAA)–related information on non-HIPAA compliant, communication channels.

Meeting Notes

This seems like one of the most basic things. After reading pages 53–57 in *LDH*, you will probably feel like the method has been far too prescriptive. The truth is this, so many teams from so many organizations simply waste a significant amount of effort and opportunity when holding meetings. It doesn't have to be this way.

Score your organization on the following set of questions. (Don't assume you know the answer, go research it.)

Score 1, 3, 5 for never, sometimes, always.

- How often do all attendees refer to previous meeting minutes? _____
- Attendees' recalled accounts of previous meetings are identical. _____
- Electronic devices never interrupt meetings. _____
- Meetings are mandatory. (For whom? When are exceptions allowed?) _____
- Our meetings make decisions. _____
- Our meetings have an agenda. _____
- Our meetings include what/who/when for follow-up. _____
- Our meeting notes are referred to at a future date. _____

Answering those questions got you thinking. Put those thoughts here.

_____

_____

_____

Take your total and divide by 40. Write your score here: _____.
What grade did you earn? _____

What next steps do you need to take? List them here or get stickies.

_____

_____

_____

Page 55 in *LDH* is a great starting point for meetings. Each point or decision should be simply summarized and viewable for all in attendance. It's highly recommended that you start with paper or whiteboard and then make the switch to electronic. It gets the team in the habit of discussing instead of publicly editing a slow typist. As mentioned on the bottom of page 56 in *LDH*, don't switch to digital unless you have a secondary screen. The reason for this is simple—the notes must always be visible to everyone in the meeting to ensure a consensus on the summary. Usually, information is being presented simultaneously. One screen cannot handle both. It becomes too clunky. There are a lot of best practices for saving and storing meeting minutes. The key is, once again, to have a system. With the level of artificial intelligence out there, even handwritten minutes can be digitized and individual words or sentences made searchable. Team members should have simple access to the proper set of minutes from anywhere. Today, that means some type of cloud-based system.

Patient Focus

You may have heard the phrase "voice of the customer." This is sometimes referred to as VoC. Let's get some things straight before we discuss this. There have been many arguments as to who is the "customer." The customer is the patient, caregiver, or family member. The customer is *never* an employee. An employee is only the customer if it is an internal process that is actually delivering something for the patient. Therefore, we referred to employees as internal stakeholders. They are the people who will be owning the process that delivers the service to the customer. As with everything in operations, the process must be repeatable and robust. This requires internal stakeholder acceptance.

At the top of page 57 in *LDH* is the following quote, "The biggest waste in creating something new is making something that nobody wants." The best way for us to know what is needed is to have a deep understanding of the customer, the patient. We can only do this if we are listening and observing, not talking or explaining. One of my favorite examples is the following story.

I was at an Executive Education program at the Jack Welch Leadership Institute in Crotonville, New York. The class was Leadership, Innovation, and Growth. In the class were senior leadership teams from multiple organizations, including one very prestigious university. The president of the university made the following statement, "We never ask students what they want. We are the educators. We always tell students what they should be doing or thinking. I guess we'll never get what we need unless we start listening to them." That president saw a systemic issue in his organization and publicly admitted it in front of his team. It was a rare display of humility from someone who had every reason to be proud. Deep patient understanding starts from the position that you don't know what you think you know.

Think about the following questions:

How much do you know about your spouse or your best friend?

Do you know their likes and dislikes?

Do you know what makes them excited?

Was that information learned on a single date or event?

These questions seem silly, but that is what we try to do with our patients. Certainly, we can pick some things up via our interaction, but we rarely talk to them about the experience because we're focused on delivering care.

Read pages 57–60 in *LDH*. There are a couple of key takeaways that need to be highlighted. Most patients are unable to clearly articulate procedural pain points. Both Henry Ford and Steve Jobs were clear that they didn't provide what their customers were asking for, but what they needed. They're both famous for stating that no one asked for an iPhone or a car. Both of those leaders had such a deep understanding of the marketplace, their consumers, and what the future needed that they made it. When finding true VoC . . .

You can't

- Ask yes/no questions
- Have them score specific areas
- Let them go on and on about how great you are and how happy they are that you are their provider

You can

- Listen instead of talk
- Record every word they say
- Suspend your judgement
- Prepare but be ready to go off script

The top of page 60 in *LDH* discusses statistically significant research before going into multiple pages of how to collect, distill, and summarize the information. We are not creating a dissertation for every project. It is not our goal to create peer-reviewed, evidence-based medicine practices. For many of the areas that you can innovate within your healthcare system, you don't need this level of detail. Remember, let's focus on process so you can focus on practicing medicine. The technique explained on pages 60–64 in *LDH* works for almost every innovation project. Let's do an exercise.

Patient Information

What insights are you trying to learn?

What geographical area are those patients from?

Where can you most easily access the patients (e.g., post-appointment, home)?

List three conversation-starting questions:

1. _____

2. _____

3. _____

Determine the best

Location _____

Interviewer _____

Time/date _____

Here is a simple spreadsheet that you can use for setting up your patient interviews.

Interviewee	Date	Time	Location	Scheduled?	Verified?	Interviewer	Questions

It may seem resource intensive, but try to have two people at every interview. Here's why: you want one person capturing the conversation and the other person focusing on the questions. The person taking notes can hand questions to the interviewer if he or she sees themes or areas that were missed. It is best practice to do an audio recording for every interview and to have it transcribed afterward. This may seem unnecessary and overkill, but it's easy for interviews to start overlapping into each other and to miss the way the patient's point was made and its context. Remember to get patient permission to record. Your legal department may have a general media release form for the patient to sign; however, if it is the same one used by marketing, you may need to modify it because you will not be using the information for advertising or externally.

Distillation

After you have collected a dozen or more hours of interviews, you must then pull out the five to ten salient points that best capture the key sentiments. Distillation can take days of work and should be divided into both individual and group effort portions. If the team itself is creating the transcription, it's easier to determine the key points. Once transcriptions are created for each interview, they should be distributed to the core team. Each team member should study the transcription and make their own notes. The team should then come together to summarize their collective findings. This can take a half a day to a full day. It seems like a lot of work. It is. But this is the foundation you need to stand out from competitors and win with patients.

On page 65 in *LDH*, one of the characters talks about creating a word cloud. I recommend you do the same thing using a website like https://www.wordclouds.com/. You can adjust the filters to remove small words or only focus on the top 50 to 100 words. You can play with colors and patterns to create a personalized, visual story.

Sometimes, during distillation, you come up with more points than can be easily organized. Frequently, this is the result of recognizing that some patient types are different than others, and they need their own representation. *LDH* refers to these as "personas." Each persona represents a discrete preference type. There is one or more major need that distinguishes one from another.

Let's use breakfast as an example. Here are some of the factors that impact breakfast choice:

- Speed of preparation
- Cost
- Healthiness
- Ease
- Familiarity
- Taste
- Amount

I'm sure you can think of others. If we look at some potential segments for breakfast eaters, we can come up with the following tree.

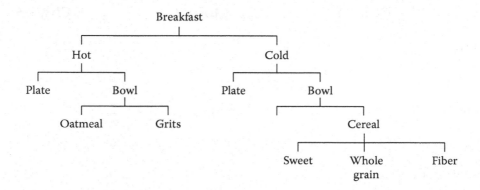

Now, we can go all the way down to the bottom where we see whole grain. At the time of this writing, there were thirteen different flavors of Cheerios. That is some serious segmentation. Pringles offers almost double the variety of flavors (twenty-two) of their hyperbolically shaped potato crisp. At large consumer product goods companies, there are individual product managers for each line. Cheerios has at least one product manager, and Pringles has at least one product manager. They are specifically focused on the segments and subsegments around the type of person who would eat their snack.

You may never get to this level, but the more research you do into your patients, the more segments or personas you will identify. You will find out which attributes make each of them unique so you can create different care models and services to address each. While most healthcare organizations don't even have the single patient defined, I recommend having no fewer than three after completing one stage of market research.

By grouping the comments and preferences, you can then create fictional characters that come to life on the walls of your innovation center. You can make a "patient" who has a name, age, gender, profession, family status, and so on. Pull out actual patient quotes and boldly highlight them. These patient personas become the foundation on which future projects are built.

Kid Persona

Pick three children who you know well, and fill out the chart.

	Child 1	**Child 2**	**Child 3**
Gender	_____	_____	_____
Ethnicity	_____	_____	_____
Interests	_____	_____	_____
Age	_____	_____	_____
Favorite food	_____	_____	_____
Music	_____	_____	_____
Play time	_____	_____	_____

If you were going to write a biographical book for each child, what would the name of each book be?

_____   _____   _____

_____   _____   _____

There is no such thing as a universal child, and there's no such thing as a universal patient. We don't have the freedom to create an infinite number of care models, so we will start with several personas and address each accordingly.

Queue

This section gives the solution for the number one reason for project delays in innovation: too many ideas/projects. Read pages 67–75 of *LDH*, highlighting statements that stick out to you.

What were the top three to five things that stood out?

_____

_____

_____

_____

_____

Key to Speed Is Maintaining Forward Progression

This will give you access to a new tool and will allow you to relate to the project queue. It is best done on a desktop computer, not your phone:

1. Type the name of your metropolitan city, state into a Google search window.
2. Click on the map on the right side of the results. (It should open in Google Maps.)
3. On the left side of the screen should be your city name. Next to it are three, short, stacked lines that open a menu.
4. Click on that menu and click Traffic. (You may have traffic shown by default. If so, leave it on.) It will show the current live traffic of your city.
5. Are there any red lines on roads? Are there associated symbols showing construction or an accident?
6. At the bottom center is a small window that says Live Traffic, and it has a down caret next to it.
7. Click on the down caret and choose Typical Traffic. This will allow you to choose a day and time of day.
8. Play with the days of the week and times of the day to see how much green (good traffic flow) and red (near standstill traffic) you can make.

Think about these questions:

What is the difference between green and red?

What causes red?

How do more vehicles, limited traffic lanes, construction, and accidents relate to projects and work?

Think about the exercise and its work implications. We know it. We hate it. Yet, somehow, we allow our innovation roadways get clogged with traffic and be impacted by things out of our control.

There is the only commodity that is the same with all people. **Time**. We all have 168 hours each week to get things done. There are 168 hours to work, sleep, exercise, do family activities, have hobbies, and hang with friends.

We have intense pressure to **do more and have more**. Fear of missing out (FOMO) packs our planner. Smartphones keep us connected 24/7. We have to do the same thing to our projects as we did to our metrics. Queueing theory tells us that wait time starts to rise dramatically after 80 percent utilization.

Let's talk innovation funnel management or vetting so we can **maintain forward progression**.

Funnel Exercise

1. **Acceptance Criteria: How do they get in the funnel?**
   a. **Who** reviews?
      i. Lower level is better.
      ii. Fewer is better.
   b. **What** is important?
      i. Finance? Time to market?
      ii. Which are mandated fixes due to previous failure? These may trump all criteria.
   c. **Weighting** system:
      i. How important is each of the criteria? Give it a weighting factor.
      ii. Test weighting with a real example.
   d. **Gradual maturation** of the project:
      i. Don't try to get the project to the finish line all at once.
      ii. Focus on what needs to be done now.
         1. Wedding—Venue versus wedding dress versus flowers.
         2. What could be delayed? Delay it.

   Lean Canvas. Don't complete a full MBA business case to determine if the project should be in the funnel.
2. **Radical Reduction: Rarely a shortage of ideas.**
   a. List *every* project (including secret ones).
   b. Use three to five of the most critical criteria.
   c. Conduct group scoring.

   • We introduce a **quality risk** when we contract or outsource. Little to no expertise in our internal systems and expectations. Zero future accountability. Who will handle warranty claims or critical fixes?
   • **Quantitative versus qualitative** assessment. Without data, it becomes a battle of who is the most politically savvy, delivering the best arguments to help their view.
   • **Strategic alignment**. Are we focused on our 3-year (and longer) goals? Let operations worry about today. Innovation is about the future. Is our funnel full of things aligned with corporate strategy or "gimme" projects.
   • **Say versus do**. Everyone pushing a project into the funnel needs to be held accountable for the arguments they use to get their project approved. Future reflection to see if the results were actually achieved minimizes office politics.
   • **Financial** impact.
   • What are your technologists working on? You need to know this. It may seem silly to ask people to track this, but until you know what they're working on, you don't know what's slowing them down.

3. **Funnel Review: When do you update?**
    a. Risk weighting **progression**:
        i. The further down the funnel, the more likely it should come out the other side.
        ii. I despise the "fail fast, fail often" advice. The goal is that no project should fail; only the options you consider for the project should fail.
        iii. However, until a project exits the funnel and is officially a project, we should be able to stop it at any time, especially because we should have given minimal effort and investment to date.
    b. **Less frequent** than more frequent:
        i. There is a tendency to want to review all the time.
        ii. There is no reason to review more than half the innovation release time.

Impact to portfolio **profitability**:
   We assume the more mature a project is, the lower the risk. This allows us to valuate that project more highly than one that is new. However, we rarely do that. It's much easier to introduce a new idea than it is to keep going with an old one.

Dynamic bottleneck:

- We don't get stuck on the same thing all the time.
- We have to consider the overlap of all projects and all resources.
- If we constantly have the same limiter, we need to fix that limiter. Remember, we're trying to maintain **forward progression**.

For the next exercise, you need to get a small group of people together who can play each role. This is fun to do with your existing team.

Project Choice Simulation

Roles

- Hospital President: Major announcement to board/community leaders now near deadline.
- Chief Marketing Officer: Made promise to major new client.
- Chief Innovation Officer: Limited resources, especially in artificial intelligence (AI).
- Chief Financial Officer: Financial planning and analysis includes all projects.
- Chief Operations Officer: Don't have capital to tool everything.
- Chief Information Officer: Already behind in technology.

Team Activity: Decide which projects remain, which are paused, and which are eliminated. You have the capacity to handle approximately two projects each year. (The project list is on the next page.)

Skip ahead to page 60, when complete continue reading below.

Four Options (Hopefully you follow #1, but teams always have rule breakers.)

1. Followed instructions: Development team had radical productivity, and resulting product release resulted in market cap doubling.
2. Worked two, kept six: Missed launch dates. Slid from market leader to #2. Stock tumbled.
3. Worked all: Sales fell. Company acquired for pennies on the dollar. Entire development team laid off.
4. Hired additional resources: Quality failure led to public class action lawsuit. Sales tanked. Company shutdown.

Those whose projects weren't completed choose a number between one and six. The following is the result of not getting their project completed.

1. Early retirement
2. Demoted
3. Kept on but on probation
4. Promoted but publicly fired in 2 years
5. Hired by competitor. Same issues.
6. Moved to Costa Rica. Beach life.

At the end . . .

What criteria did the team agree to?

_____

_____

_____

_____

What information is needed to make better decisions?

_____

_____

_____

_____

What other issues did you face?

_____

_____

_____

_____

Project List

Fifty person-years (py) of capacity per annum.

1. Project 1
   a. Major announcement 6 months ago at an analyst meeting regarding new AI-driven product offering
   b. 25 percent complete
   c. 30 py
2. Project 2
   a. Potential new large client switching from competitor; new project key to getting them onboard
   b. 50 percent complete
   c. 20 py
3. Project 3
   a. Halo project that will demonstrate ability to release the highest-performing product on the market across multiple, global segments
   b. 50 percent complete
   c. 40 py
4. Project 4
   a. Bundled projects replace lowest-margin products in the portfolio; key to increasing earnings per share (EPS) over next six quarters; already in financial projections
   b. 25 percent complete
   c. 25 py
5. Project 5
   a. Project to renovate factory to near total automation to reduce labor costs; minimal impact to new product development
   b. 0 percent complete
   c. 10 py
6. Project 6
   a. Project to shift from data lake to data hubs to enhance deep learning capabilities (for use on all future clients)
   b. 10 percent complete
   c. 30 py

Methodologies

There are a number of great innovation methodologies: Lean Product Development, Agile, Design Thinking, Lean Startup, Design for Six Sigma, and more. Each of the methodologies has advantages and disadvantages. Both the pros and cons are dynamic and based on the type and maturity of development that is happening. Newer, progressive techniques demand fast iteration and rapid learning cycles. There is an overused and often abused mantra of "fail fast, fail often."

Getting it done right is far better than getting it done fast; however, if you're going so slow that your solution is outdated by the time it's introduced to the market, then you aren't going fast enough.

Having studied multiple industries with a wide variety of innovation maturity, this book was written specifically for healthcare. Although most industries could benefit from the contents, the custom focus of this book for the healthcare environment makes it a competitive advantage for those who implement its practices. The tools in this section have been found to be highly effective in launching accurate, quick, robust, innovative services in healthcare.

Pugh

One of the worst types of innovations is when a person brings a solution without a need. Working backward always creates problems. Other times, innovators will work on things that are necessary or they are trying to be helpful, but they didn't consider the end user.

The best way to ensure appropriateness is to enter every innovation project in a cycle of discovery. Over time, we ask the right questions, and we learn more. Our solution becomes more and more mature with each decision that we made.

The best innovators know that individual ideas must get better and that the vast majority of the innovation process is made up of little decisions. Each of those little decisions could have gone one of many directions. There is a methodology that uses an approach called "set-based design." In it, the "set" is the totality of an acceptable performance region. This region is bounded by trade-off curves determined through testing. On one side of the curve is unacceptable performance and on the other is acceptable. It can take years to develop proper trade-off curves, and like everything else, they change as consumer tastes and preferences change. One doesn't need set-based design to benefit. One must simply learn how to consider multiple options in a group environment and make decisions in an environment that thrives on that. The Pugh matrix is a tool that enables just that. Read pages 75–80 of *LDH*.

This was a fairly straightforward example. This tool can be used in situations from simple to complex. There are two blank matrices below that you can use to practice. Let's start with something in your personal life and then try one in your professional arena.

Lunch

In your personal life, the decision could be as simple as where you are going to eat lunch to where you will take a vacation to something more complex like what job you will take next.

1. Fill in the title of your decision first.
2. List three factors that will impact your decision, and list them across the top.
3. Come up with three options for your decision, and list them down the first column.
4. Decide if you want to use numbers or letters for ranking (1, 3, 5 or H, M, L).
5. Rank each possible solution by factor.
6. Score each option. (It could be 3.5 or medium-high.)

Lunch	Criteria 1	Criteria 2	Criteria 3
Option 1			
Option 2			
Option 3			
New Option			

During your scoring, you may have thought about a factor you forgot, or you may have thought of a new option or derivative that you hadn't originally considered.

Go back and put those on the chart and complete the additional scoring. Total the scores once again. Challenge yourself to create this matrix again at home and complete it with a family member. Do the scores change at all? Were there other factors or options you hadn't considered?

Every time you add a person, they will take a slightly different position. Some factors will be more important to that person. The discussion on the scoring gets more complicated. Ultimately, you may need to have a decision-maker to break a tie or choose the best option simply because two seem equally attractive.

When you feel comfortable, repeat this exercise with a colleague from work. Pick a simple decision you are trying to make together. Follow the same steps as before.

Answer the following questions:

How does the exercise make you feel?

What did the tool make easier?

What did the tool make more difficult?

How easy was it to come up with an initial list of options?

Was it easy to decide on the factors?

How could your organization benefit from the tool?

In what meeting could you introduce the tool?

Is there a leader in your organization whom you should share the tool with first?

Organizations can benefit most from using this tool during their regular operating mechanisms in which decisions about solutions or directions must be made and multiple options are being considered.

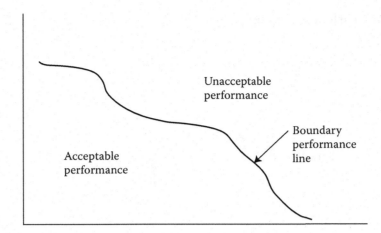

Analytical Hierarchy Process

Now, what happens if your list contains ten to fifteen things or possibly many more than that? The Pugh matrix begins to exponentially lose its effectiveness the more options it must consider. This is where the analytical hierarchy process (AHP) shines. In particular, this tool is prioritizing and waiting for patient or internal stakeholder needs.

Again, we go back to the theme that "creating something nobody wants" is the biggest waste in innovation. It is extremely rare to see a project that has as many resources dedicated to it as the leader thinks is necessary. Therefore, the innovation process itself becomes a series of trade-offs, choosing the best alternative given the factors. This was demonstrated with the previous tool. In all likelihood, cost, time, or technology readiness will limit the solutions you employ to solve your patient needs. As such, you need to know where to focus your energy for maximum impact. There is a simple exercise in marketing research in which survey respondents are asked to distribute $100 across multiple options. For instance, if we are choosing lunch restaurants and the factors are cost, speed, and variety, the customer can choose how to distribute the hundred dollars among the three. They may choose $50, $25, $25. They could choose $70, $30, $0, or any other combination. The market researcher can average the amount of dollars for each item from all respondents to determine which one of the attributes is most important to the customer. The innovation team should then focus on delivering solutions that address those needs in the prioritized order. Let's say the customers for this restaurant chose speed. Whatever new recipe ideas they come up with, they should be able to be prepared faster.

The AHP allows an innovation team to take a long list of options and accurately allocate 100 percentage points in a fair, systematic approach. Team members, each having immersed themselves in the patient experience through interviews, transcription analysis, and distillation, should be able to represent the patient segments as the tool is used. The tool works much like a round-robin tournament. Every item competes against every other item, accumulating scores that will be summed up at the end.

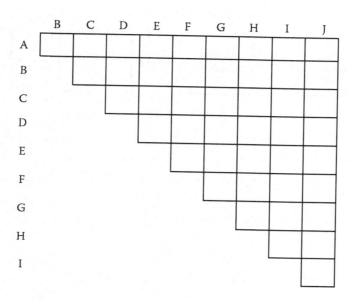

Discussing just two at a time allows the team to focus and ensures critical dialogue that yields solid results. You may be tempted to just allocate the 100 points against the list itself. To do so suppresses the intense debate that makes AHP so successful. Resist the urge, and use the model in the book. Using this tool has a bit of a learning curve. Read pages 80–86 of *LDH* to gain an understanding of typical issues faced.

Failure Modes and Effects Analysis

Technically, instead of Failure Modes and Effects Analysis (FMEA), it's usually a PFMEA, or *Process* Failure Modes and Effects Analysis, but since most services are process based, the *P* was removed for simplicity.

This tool is the basic one for ensuring robustness of the process. If we are going to create a new service model, we want to make sure every step of the process is done well. If any steps of the process fail, then those upstream will be affected, as they will not be allowed to continue. A queue will start to build, frustrating providers, staff, and patients. Each step should have the highest likelihood of being 100% complete per the plan.

Sandwich Maker

Let's use the following template for a simple example: making a sandwich.

1. Decide type
2. Collect ingredients
3. Prepare bread
4. Assemble sandwich

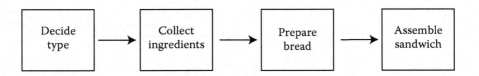

Now let's consider a potential failure mode for each step. I'm sure you could imagine a few other options.

1. You can't decide which type of sandwich.
2. You're out of one or more ingredients.
3. You have one slice of bread and one heel, and you don't like the heel.
4. You only have a limited amount of the main ingredient, and you drop it on the floor.

Second, we assess the likelihood of each failure.

1. You can never figure out what sandwich you want.
2. You keep your cupboards well stocked.
3. Everybody in your house eats sandwiches.
4. You're always doing three things at a time.

You can imagine your own scenarios, but each likelihood will impact your ability to make your sandwich.

Next, let's decide what the impact of that failure would be on the sandwich-making process.

1. You can't eat it as fast as you want.
2. The sandwich will be different from the one you wanted.
3. You have to decide if it's worth making a sandwich or not.
4. You don't believe in the 3-second rule.

Some of those have a bigger impact on your sandwich, while others . . . not so much.

We can now move on to failure detection. This is the process ability to not have a failure get discovered. Let's look at each of the four.

1. You will know when you decide the sandwich type.
2. Your meat and produce drawers in your refrigerator are packed, making it hard to tell what you have or don't have.
3. Your bread box is transparent, showing a single loaf of bread.
4. You are very meticulous during your sandwich assembly.

We can give high, medium, and low scores for each of the steps during each of the phases. Low equals one, medium equals three, and high equals five. Next, we can multiply the scores for each number.

Finally, we have a total score for each step. The higher the score, the greater is our need to introduce a countermeasure to prevent failure.

For instance, if you always eat peanut butter and jelly sandwiches, then you don't have to worry about deciding between multiple options. However, if your whole family eats them, and you could be out of one or more ingredients, then that has a high failure mode possibility. We could make it very simple by having a spare peanut butter hidden somewhere or by quickly scanning for ingredients before deciding what type of sandwich to make. When you create a countermeasure, you should re-score each process step, trying to get the total number as low as possible.

FMEA

Use the below template for a work process. Keep it simple for this exercise. You can make your own spreadsheet for a full-blown analysis of a formal process. It will be dozens and dozens, if not hundreds, of lines.

Process Step	Possible Failure	Likelihood of Failure	Impact of Failure	Detection Hiding	Total	Countermeasure

Since these are starting points for your toolbox, learn them, use them, reflect on use, and then adapt, create, and add others. Repeat. You should be seeing a theme here. It's the scientific method. The operational excellence community calls it PDCA (plan, do, check, act). With any repeated process, you need to create the standard, see how effective it is, reflect, and modify. Repeat.

Chapter 4

RED Framework

Think back to Chapter 2 when both the art and science of systematic innovation were discussed. Pages 91–93 in *Lean Design in Healthcare (LDH)* talk about the art of innovation. It's very hard to develop this side. Most people have a natural ability, and further developing that ability yields great results. The percentage of the population that can do this is small. Think about any talented creative position: musician, artist, or graphic designer. It comes far more easily for the best ones. Sure, anyone can learn some basic techniques, but if you only have one person on your innovation team, you want that person's "artistry" to be as high as possible. We are going to apply the "scientific" process that will allow them to truly excel—in a systematic way within an organization.

There is a phrase at the very bottom of page 92 in *LDH*. Write it down here:

_____

_____

_____

or by the alternate phrase the coach used at the top of page 93:

_____

_____

_____

Best Innovating.

You have your highest chance of doing this if you do the three bullet points right before the section we just read. Find them in the book, and list them here.

1.

2.

3.

Write down one of your hobbies that you are fairly good at. This could be birding, gardening, cooking, fishing, cycling, or whatever.

_____

Now write down three techniques that the average person most likely would not know about your hobby.

Item   **Importance**

1. _____   _____

2. _____   _____

3. _____   _____

Beside each of those three points, write down why each is important.

When you first learned your hobby, you didn't know these. Describe what happened after you learned these skills.

Are there any additional skills that you have heard about that you would like to learn?

What would learning the skills allow you to do?

It might seem basic, but the same principle applies in innovation. The more we learn, the more you are able to do and the higher level you're able to perform at.

Regardless of your aptitude toward it, if you have never created a new product or service from scratch, consider yourself an innovation novice. This would be just like when you began your hobby. You had an interest, but you had beginner results. The more time you spend learning and trying, the better you become. The same applies for innovation. Look at the first three points listed earlier from page 92 in *LDH*. Those are three skill sets we are going to work on to be better innovators.

Fact Collection

Read pages 93–94 in *LDH*. The key here is immersion. You don't collect the best facts by dabbling, you do it by completely immersing yourself into the situation.

Sure, you can start with a Google search or with some reports, but eventually you will want to become the expert regarding your patients and communicating that with your organization. Facts-shared-passionately is the most powerful tool an innovator has.

What data can you collect to prove your view?

_____

_____

_____

How can you collect it?

_____

_____

_____

Pattern Recognition

Read pages 94–96 in *LDH*. For this skill, you need to be able to connect seemingly disparate ideas and concepts. It helps to be able to slice information a bunch of different ways. It's good to have someone who loves to play with data on the team. They can take the information and create a whole bunch of different infographics. It's rare to have more than a couple of people who can do this on your team. Give them the work, and then let them show you what they come up with. It is rarely the most obvious method of presenting the data that becomes the most beneficial.

Who are good candidates for this?

_____

_____

_____

What data can you give them to look for patterns?

_____

_____

_____

Solution Awareness

Read pages 96–98 in *LDH*. You need to be able to fully leverage all of your knowledge. It's best if you keep up to date in several areas. You can do this through reading magazines, listening to podcasts, watching documentaries and YouTube videos, or a bunch of other things. The key is to absorb information from a multitude of services so that when you do look at a given set of data, you can pull from it.

Think about where you currently collect information. List them:

_____

_____

_____

What areas are missing?

_____

_____

_____

What sources could you add?

_____

_____

_____

Evolution of the Crazy

Read page 98 in *LDH*. In a 2012 *Fast Company* article, a Pixar executive discussed how their movies go from "suck to not suck" and beyond. They perfectly describe the evolution of the crazy concept: creativity, candid feedback, and iteration. Innovation teams that can create the same culture well also have great success. But to do that, you need to start off with some fairly outlandish ideas. You can't start with something simple and turn it into something complex; it almost never works that way. You have to start with something that seems ridiculous or completely silly, and then figure out how to make it work best.

What problems are you most passionate about fixing?

_____

_____

_____

Who have you shared this with?

_____

_____

_____

One of the most helpful elements of systematic innovation is to have an agreed framework that the organization follows. Like everything else in this book, it should be continually updated and improved. However, to get started, we must have something. The RED (research, exploration, delivery) framework was created based on dozens of client experiences. It is the most effective way for a healthcare organization to get started in systematic innovation. If, up until this point, your innovation has been ad hoc or run by the information technology (IT) department, this will be quite different. In fact, you may get a significant amount of pushback. People who argue for something other than the RED framework are operating myopically. They only know the world they have been subjected to and their own personal experiences. Far more often than not, they lack depth and an understanding of the myriad of available options, let alone the pros and cons of each. This work has been done for you already.

We use the RED framework every day in our lives without even realizing it. Anytime we make a decision about lunch or where to go on vacation, we use the RED framework. We don't need a formal process for doing those two things. We can do them with one or two people. However, when we are running a project that involves seven or more functions and could impact hundreds or thousands of employees, we need to follow a formal framework. It's the only way that everybody stays on the same page and works on the appropriate task. A framework also ensures that no steps were skipped. Skipping steps results in costly fixes later.

A major assumption for the RED framework is that you have already developed a queue, a funnel of project ideas, and that you have a system in place for approving or stopping them (see Chapter 3).

Please understand that an idea coming out of the funnel does not have to have any more definition than an idea. In fact, if a solution is already proposed, then the RED framework has been skipped. "Let's switch to an Epic EMR, implement a Kareo Telemedicine package, or build an ambulatory surgical center" are examples of statements about solutions that skip the RED framework. Because most healthcare delivery organizations do not have an innovation team, they rely heavily on medical device and software companies to propose solutions. Another traditional approach is to just copy what others are doing. Many of these "strategic initiatives" are tackled without a deep understanding of their market, without knowing what it takes to be competitive, and without researching the best alternatives for the employee and the patient. Yet, it is done again and again. Why? Because it seems easier. And it is. At first.

Read pages 99–104 in *LDH*. Atkins, paleo, keto. Just like diet trends, there are innovation trends. Design thinking and Agile rule the mindshare right now. Everybody is scrambling to figure out how to use them at their organizations. Before that was Lean Product Development and Design for Six Sigma. Most diet trends have found that an excessive amount of high glycemic index carbohydrates can be harmful and can lead to poor health and/or chronic conditions.

Similarly, every innovation methodology knows that there must be a product definition phase and a design/testing phase before release. Every methodology has a specific focus and shines in one area brighter than the others. The RED framework was created so that an organization can have zero experience innovating and still produce great results. There are a few keys to successful implementation. You must determine the length of time that your organization can be patient, and you must commit to learning (and adjusting based on the latest information).

It may seem a bit archaic to rely on paper on walls, but it still remains the simplest, yet powerful visual storyteller available. There are organizations that create incredible video summaries created by graphical geniuses. If that's what's needed to convince your executives, then by all means, do it. However, you can usually get away with a lot less.

Research

Read pages 104–109 in *LDH*. The key to this stage is finding it what you don't know and then using that information to discover what else you don't know. Answer the questions on the following page.

Research Questions

What problem do you need data to prove?

What in-house data can support that?

Who can collect it?

What's happening outside your organization?

Who can collect that?

What are high-growth competitors doing?

What do patients really think?

How do they live?

Come up with a list of questions you need answered.

1.

2.

...

X.

Next, it's time to use the analytic hierarchy process (AHP) tool introduced in the last chapter to prioritize your list so you can focus on the most important things. Not because it's always needed at this step, but for practice.

Order of Importance (copy results here)

1.

2.

...

X.

Now it's time to consider the entire body of knowledge with your team and see if you can do some pattern recognition.

	B	C	D	E	F	G	H	I	J
A									
B									
C									
D									
E									
F									
G									
H									
I									

Exploration

Read pages 109–112 in *LDH*. This stage is all about creating solutions for a list of prioritized needs. The basic building block of a solution is a feature. A feature is simply a characteristic that addresses any combination of a part with its corresponding single or multiple needs. A feature can be a stand-alone or it can be combined with other features for a larger release. Think of features as elements that your marketing team could promote on social media, billboards, or in emails. Think two- to three-word descriptors.

Feature Identification and Performance

Let's say we have interviewed or surveyed many patients and have found a segment of single moms who are struggling to take time off work to take their kid(s) to appointments. This could be related to a chronic condition or the follow-up from an exacerbation. After much consideration and debate, you create a feature called "Mom Friendly." There are a bunch of solutions that could fall under this broad category. They could include anything from hours to location to online assistance. Details to follow. For now, *Mom Friendly* is our starting point. Next is performance.

Feature performance is how well the feature delivers against a need. It's easy to understand in terms of a car that gets a certain miles per gallon of gas compared to another car. But what about healthcare? The example in the book talks about wait time in the emergency room. Your performance is only good if it's better than the competition. You have to decide what good performance looks like for the *Mom Friendly* feature.

Your team debates and decides that the winning performance level means that a professional working mom doesn't have to take any time off (zero time off is your performance level) of work to take her kid(s) to an appointment. You look at the demographics of your ZIP Code and determine that the average commute is 25 minutes. You assume an average starting time of 8 a.m. and an average ending time of 5 p.m. for most professional jobs. This tells you the appointments must be complete before 7:30 a.m. or start after 5:30 p.m. (Monday through Friday). Through conversations with moms, you also found that final preparation for the upcoming week, on Sunday evening, would be a great time for at least providing advice to a desperate mom.

Possible Subsegment

What if the segment included moms who didn't work in a professional role? They were in hospitality services or manufacturing, and their hours were less predictable? What type of information would you need?

_____

_____

_____

Mom Friendly is a single feature. To populate the next tool requires at least one of these features but could include as many as ten or more.

After considering the age of new moms in your area, let's say that you decide "Digital" is another feature. You want to give moms the ability to access a solution from their phone. Any critical thing that can be phone accessible would be way easier than synchronous phone calls.

For the next feature, think. When going through the interview transcripts, you will remember seeing a lot of complaints about getting and picking up prescriptions and medication, including over-the-counter ones. You know that moms want symptom management and treatment as quickly as possible for their children. After much arguing, you decide on a feature called "Meds Now," a way to get medication to the mom or her child in less than an hour. We don't worry about how at this point. We're defining what it means to win with single moms. It may be applicable to other segments, but they're not the current focus.

You now have three features. Each one needs to be fully developed, but first let's look at our example using some helpful tools.

There are two more tools introduced in the exploration phase: the Quality Functional Deployment (QFD) and the Prototype Process (PP). Let's cover each briefly.

QFD

Pages 112–113 in *LDH*.

There isn't a lot of information on the QFD tool in the book. Often, the tool can get in the way of what its original intent was. The QFD can become so complex because it was originally designed to be a multitiered tool. Search online for "House of Quality" for examples. The main purpose for using the tool in healthcare innovation is to ensure that we have solutions for all of the problems and that all of the problems are being addressed by a feature. It's a simple, one-page grid that quickly lets us know we're covering everything well.

"*Where to Give*" as an example for immunizations.
Our needs are easily accessible, day schedulable, and delivered by appropriate licensure.
Our features can be at the worksite, electronic scheduling, and delivered by RNs. Here, in this simple example, there is a 1:1 ratio between needs and solutions.

QFD		Needs		
		Access	**Schedule**	**Licensure**
Features	Worksite	X		
	Electronic Scheduling		X	
	RNs			X

The more complex a new service model gets, the more Needs a single feature might address. For instance, one of the assumptions behind an electronic medical record (EMR) was that it could not just record the note, but orders could be made, patient history could be tracked, and billing could be more automated. (However, it added significant administrative burden to the physician.)

After reflection and intense discussion, your team is quite comfortable with *Mom Friendly*, but how do you go from a feature to something that works? Keep reading!

Feature Creation and Testing

Going back to the Mom Friendly example, you look at your historical data and see that most kids treated on Mondays or with same-day appointments have a pattern. The pattern you see is that a physician is rarely needed. In fact, virtually all of the appointments could be handled by a nurse or a nurse practitioner. In addition, 25% of the cases could have been handled strictly over the phone.

You know your organization offers urgent care at several locations, but they would be quite inconvenient for many of your "working moms" as the hours are still not adequate. The innovation team decides to create a "Mom Clinic" that includes a triage line.

"Meds Now" is an Uber-like medicine delivery service. The location where the medicine is being delivered determines whether a nurse or a courier will deliver the medication. Throughout initial feasibility, your team decides that this feature can only be delivered with a small additional fee. You decide to give moms a $10 per month option for this service.

	Process step 1	Process step 2	...	Process step X
Purpose				
Location				
Patient				
Resources				
Equipment				
IT/EMR				
Information				
Time				
FMEA #1				

Your job is to populate the prototype process using any one of our examples or your own example. The key is to think in discrete steps. What is the first thing that would need to be done? That goes at the top of column one. You can then think about all of the "ingredients" for each of the rows that are necessary to deliver that first step. You can repeat this process for each column until you have fully populated the chart. Sometimes you may only have three or four steps, and other times you may have fifteen. It all depends on the complexity of the new process.

Feature creation and development on the PP tool can take some time. You need to involve every function that has a part in the solution. There will be negotiations and trade-offs required to get each part right. It may require new software, hardware, personnel, or facilities.

Next, you must test your new process to see how it works. The first few times through should be with your team only, just walking through the process with one of you acting as the patient. This will allow you to work out any major bugs before you involve a patient. Once you are confident with that, you can begin patient testing of the feature. This requires a considerable amount of coordination, but it should be remembered that it is still an experiment at this point. Many of the steps can be manual with rudimentary techniques and tools. For instance, this could require manual scheduling and paper being used instead of software. The major goal of the first round of testing is to see if the process works and is addressing the needs of the patient. The team should take time after each round of experimentation to reflect and make adjustments to the process with an eye on optimization of technique.

Additional rounds can be added while still in the exploration phase, depending on how long it takes to achieve the desired performance. Eventually, it will need to be formalized for all patients in the next phase of the RED framework, delivery.

Delivery

Read pages 117–118 in *LDH*. This stage is about preparing the innovation for launch. Robustness is key. This phase requires heavy involvement from operations. Also, you should fully leverage your performance excellence (PE) team so they can leverage the basic principles of Lean when establishing the standard work for the organization. Standard work will be the recipe for the staff and providers to follow in the new service model. Ultimately, it will dictate all the critical points and techniques necessary to address the pain points we discovered during patient interviews and observation.

Pages 120–121 in *LDH* discuss the concept of a minimum viable product (MVP). A lot of organizations fail to properly use this technique and cause far more harm than good. It's critical to understand that an MVP should be a prototype, and not something available to the patient. If it is made available to the patient, it should only be in a testing capacity. Final release means all the kinks have been worked out. The PE team has approved it, and Operations becomes responsible for it.

Pages 121–123 in *LDH* talk about failing. Suki's line near the top of page 122 says it best. A lot of organizations have a severe phobia about failing. This is understandable. They don't want to lose the investment of time and money that they have made in the project. Executives know how limited resources are, and they want everything to be a success. Innovation projects can range from mild to "betting the farm." The larger the stakes are, the higher the pressure to not fail. It would be wise to practice the advice at the top of page 122 in *LDH*. The key is to recognize when an idea has failed, to get over it, and to come up with an alternative. Every next step in the maturation of a project should be nebulous until that step is reached. Unless somebody has already defined it, you should be considering multiple options. All but one of those options will fail.

Sometimes, you get too far and realize that the project won't work. This could be because capital dried up, it could be because the technical resource source isn't available or that you can't hire the people you were expecting to use or anything else. Each of the people responsible for those functions should be monitoring their own feasibility and defining only what is possible from their perspective.

Failure should be dealt with swiftly. Too many times, a leader will keep a project alive because of the sunk cost. But that's just it—that money is already spent and gone. Let it go. There is a high probability that you will continue to waste resources by keeping the project alive. Follow your intuition, but present with facts. Cancel projects when it's clear they won't succeed. Each organization can decide how it addresses failure. While some companies actually celebrate it, the minimum is to not punish teams for failing.

Chapter 5

Reflection

Chapter 5 of *Lean Design in Healthcare (LDH)* has so much behind-the-scenes information baked into the conversation. It focuses on a few major issues. The reality is, many of the scenarios in Chapter 5 could be entire books themselves. This workbook was created so that we could dive into each area a little bit deeper and hopefully prevent some things or enable some things related to what was read in the book.

Mom Friendly

As you were reading the "Mom Friendly" section in Chapter 4 of this workbook, you had to have some thoughts regarding your own organization. This is clearly a very simple example with a very simple solution. However, it is simple ideas like this that never see the light of day for numerous reasons. Take some time and complete the following reflection about your own organization for this example.

Make It Real

What is your role at your organization?

From your role's perspective, what do you think about the Mom Friendly feature?

What is your perspective as a patient?

Who in your organization would like it? Why?

Who in your organization would be against it? Why?

What elements of it could you apply in your organization?

Who would you need to talk to in order to get somebody behind it?

What elements would be applicable for dual-income families?

Which employers in your area would benefit?

Which payers could you negotiate higher reimbursements for it?

What would it do to improve access for higher-acuity issues during the week?

Design Thinking

The dialogue on pages 128–129 in *LDH* took a definitive position with design thinking. It starts with the innovation leader taking a very strong stance, thankful that her competitors would do design thinking instead of systematic innovation. The rest of the innovation team joins in and takes little cracks at design thinking workshops. The truth is this: something is better than nothing. Just remember, whenever you outsource a particular skill set, you are allowing that vendor to represent you. It's highly unlikely that they will be closer to the patient base than you are. They will inevitably bring in their own biases and opinions based on what they have seen, quite possibly for markets very different from your own. On top of that, there are a multitude of vendors that are offering design thinking workshops. Some have very limited healthcare delivery work. Just be aware of who you're partnering with for this crucial definition phase. Be extremely leery of companies that sell the very services for the outputs of the design thinking workshops. Any vendor leading with digital transformation or user experience should also be a red flag. They are out to sell a solution and not discover what may truly be most beneficial to your organization. Think about all the software companies that promised significant efficiency gain, yet your chief information officer and chief financial officer haven't shown a return on investment to back it up.

Pet Projects

In a resource-limited environment, distraction kills productivity more than anything. Read pages 129–132 in *LDH*. This story is one that has been played again and again at organizations. The key distinguishing element is what the leader does or doesn't do. Perhaps the leader is at fault for propagating a pet project. Pet projects are distractions that rarely yield the best use of innovation resources.

The keyword is focus. Great leaders come through times of limited resources leveraging focus more than any other tool. This means that everything has to be visible—in the lowest level all the way to the highest level. If resources are not limited, pet projects, skunk works, or whatever you prefer to call them will creep in. Stay vigilant against them.

What projects are ongoing but are unofficial? (Top 3 taking resources)

Project   Champion

_____   _____

_____   _____

_____   _____

What impacts do you think they're having on strategic initiatives?

_____

_____

_____

Where Organizations Win or Fail

The purpose of this workbook is to get systematic innovation going in your organization. Hopefully, you don't feel like you need to be a top leader in the business to do so. Any leader at any level of the organization can implement this. The greater your success, the higher the likelihood for expansion. This book is meant to be a recipe card for you.

Leadership Support

Think back to the leadership roles identified in Chapter 1. It's hard not to push this point too hard. Leadership is the foundation of success. Get a sponsor, even if it has to be off the radar for now. (Yes, we just coached against pet projects.) Your organization needs a formal system to handle the funnel and the priorities. That means getting the right people on board. Don't use any resources until you get enough supporters. Certainly, don't start working on any projects until you have the basics in place. Before the basics is leadership support. You want a wild, vocal champion.

Operations

You have to find an ally in operations, even if you are the boss. Tomorrow looks very different from today. Anytime you change operations, you disrupt the norm that they are already struggling to meet performance goals for. In fact, your innovation may help them better achieve their goals, but they still don't like it. Just remember, the patients' needs should outweigh operational needs as long as profitability remains the same or improves. The worst-case scenario would be if your operations director doesn't like any of your ideas and provides strong pushback among their sphere of influence. If necessary, partner with any supporter in an operational role to begin with. Sit down and have a chat with them.

Go back and look at the Stakeholder Exercise (page 1–5). Who are the critical people for the two aforementioned areas? Put stars next to their names. Set up a semi-recurring meeting with them, even if it's just coffee. Start sharing your ideas informally. Build momentum there.

Discover the answers to the following questions:

What major operational issues do you face?

Which things have you tried to fix them?

How open are you to new approaches to address your issues?

What have you been trying to fix forever that you haven't been able to?

How willing are you to support experiments to help improve your operations?

Other thoughts?

If you get a good sense from these questions that you can help and partner with them, that may be where you want to start. If you feel a bad vibe, table it with that person.

Coaching

Consulting or coaching services can seem to be very expensive. On the surface, books and seminars appear to be significantly cheaper and nearly as effective. Top organizations use books and seminars as a springboard to informal or formal coaching. Informal coaching occurs when an organization contacts another to exchange best practice ideas. Formal coaching is when a company or individual is hired specifically for their innovation expertise. The bottom line is that you need knowledge transfer from an expert to you. You didn't get to your role in delivering healthcare merely by reading books or taking classes. You had intensive rounds of clinicals side-by-side with an instructor. Fortunately, this won't require the same level of hands-on training before results roll in. However, it does require some. Do some research, and populate the following chart. Use that to present to the steering committee.

Organization	Claim to Fame	Healthcare Innovation Experience

Technology

Technology itself is never an answer. It certainly should never be the lead dancer. It should always follow. Don't let vendors sell you their software or hardware packages without understanding the real patient problems you are facing. There is almost always a simpler and cheaper solution available. You should be creating requests for proposals (RFPs) from your work and not taking sales calls from medical device makers or software firms. Every expenditure should be made with a comprehensive view of the patient and provider workflow.

Challenge

If *LDH* or this workbook provided even a shred of inspiration for you to try this at your organization, take a leap. Do something now. Get a small group of like-minded individuals at your organization together to discuss it. Take a half-day or a full-day retreat to answer the following questions.

Why do systematic innovation?

What's happening now?

What could the future look like?

Conclusion

The End. A lot of people have gotten to the end of the book and said, "Is that it? You ended with a cliffhanger?" Yes, I did. *LDH* is about putting the basics in place. It was never intended to be comprehensive or be wrapped up with a mountain of research. As an Enneagram Type Five, *Investigator*, I find data critical. The more, the merrier. However, as with all of my successful endeavors, data and the didactic only go so far. At some point, you have to do. Do something! After reading the book and completing the workbook, it's time for you to formally start your innovation journey. There is more than enough in this book to keep you busy for 1–3 years. In fact, I have some clients that have been using these basics for 5 or more years. If you need more convincing, more data, or actual case studies, this book was never for you. But I don't believe that will be the case for the vast majority of people who read it. You want to do something. You're ready to do something. With these two publications, you are fully equipped to start. Yes, it's a risk, but it's a risk worth taking. It'll be hard, but you'll love it. Healthcare needs people like you to take the leap. It's hard to imagine the number of people whose lives will be positively impacted because you did.

If you need more information or help, reach out to those with experience, including myself by emailing me at adam@adzmikl.com or by going to my website https://adammward.com/.

Index